The

Power

of 8:

Our Unique Journey

Forward

In my lifetime I have had the opportunity to work and see various communities grow and be shaped because of financial opportunities. As God has placed me in a position of employment in the insurance industry, that afforded me the sight of seeing Asian Americans and other groups be successful in coming together to share and/or build wealth by investing in themselves and each other as a group.

I thought, what a brilliant idea! In addition to my insurance career, I was serving as secretary and assistant to a local Pastor and Church that I saw as being somewhat successful. After much prayer, meditation, apprehension and even fear, I decided to take a great leap of faith in my own community and approach a group of people with the idea of investing in ourselves. It was my desire to approach people from various age groups, backgrounds, and educational levels.

Twenty-five plus years later it has been a thrill, and a learning experience as I witnessed the growth of those that took the challenge and are still in the race. It saddened me at that time as it does now, to discover the lack of knowledge, lack of desire and fear to put in the work it takes to be successful in the world of financial opportunities. Blessed be to God that eight of us took the torch and have continued to run with it. We call ourselves *"The Power of Eight"*.

We have learned how to invest, capitalize, teach, inspire and encourage each other and others on how to come through in good times and in tough times. If you are interested in an adventure of a lifetime of self-growth and financial opportunities, then this is the book for you ....

Mary F. Tuft

Organizer, Founder, Learner

<u>DEDICATION</u>

This book is dedicated to all investment groups, book clubs or any group of people striving to achieve success and empowerment for each member or partner they are connected with.

And to our Creator, Sustainer, Provider and Protector, Jesus Christ our Lord.

ACKNOWLEDGEMENTS

Unique Enterprises would most certainly like to take the opportunity to thank our children and grandchildren for sharing us and for giving us the mental, physical, financial, and emotional space to do all we do to leave behind a legacy for them and generations to come. We would like to thank all our loved ones who have helped and supported us in both large and small ways. Our deepest gratitude to all of the former members that started on this journey with us and stand in the wings to see us succeed in this endeavor.

We would like to acknowledge authors, Mirthell Bazemore, Geanell Gaines Robinson and Catherine "Toni" Dukes for their support and encouragement as well as Diedra "Dee" Ward who provided editing support and gave another look to our book.

Last, but most definitely not least, Unique Enterprises would like to acknowledge and thank our founder and visionary, Mary Tuft, for allowing God to use her to birth and see a group of people do what He says we can do. "I can do all things through Christ who strengthens me" (Philippians 4:13).

Table of Contents

Chapter I
<u>The Beginning</u>

Most fairy tales begin with "once upon a time", or "in a land far away", but this is not a fairytale, and the land is as close as your imagination. The story is a physical, mental, financial and spiritual journey, so let's start as The Good Book [1] says "In the beginning."

This story tells how a group of people, young and old, of means or without means, not limited to any particular racial, social, religious or financial background, can come together for economic empowerment in and among themselves and their communities.

In January 1994, the owner of a small hat shop in Oakland, California, a minority single mother of two, had the vision to form an investment group to empower individuals in her circle and their families, to embark upon a journey toward homeownership. She wanted to encourage them to think about what legacy to leave their children to build upon long after our time on this earth is over. She was ever mindful of Proverbs 13:22a that says "A good man leaves an inheritance to his children's children..." Being a person that was forever curious of other communities, she modeled her idea after what she saw in the Asian Community where they would pool their disposable income together for the purpose of helping each other. Now, this business proprietor is African American, born and raised in the state of Mississippi. We know the prevailing attitude is that "black folk cannot come together", nor can they work together unless forced to do so by other people – hence slavery! We know this ain't true, right? So she called together 30 other individuals who she thought were serious and open minded. She looked for positive, family-oriented people, friends, and business associates. Those who wanted to join her in this vision to combine forces, resources, ideas, time and expertise were more than welcome to attend. She realized that many different types of people would be needed to increase our economic base and to make our surroundings a better place to live, work and play.

Keep in mind that this story took place prior to the internet as we know it today. So whereas this process may sound primitive now, it wasn't at that time. A meeting was scheduled and held at the organizer's hat shop and everybody was invited to come and hear the idea for the launching of this investment opportunity.

Normally when marketing an idea to any group of people you can usually count on 10% return on the invitations. Amazingly, of the 30 invitations, 23 people came to the meeting to hear the Vision (later known as "Business Plan 94") and eat the snacks. As part of the plan the suggestion was made that everyone invest $1,000. Another meeting was scheduled, and NO, not one of us brought the $1000 seed money. Since this investment group concept was a novel idea in our community, some invitees came to the meeting to inquire. Some came to learn more about the Vision, while others came just because they were invited and, of course, there were those that came to gawk and had nothing else to do.

After laying out the Vision, all types of questions were raised around how this group would work and what would be the focus, etc. The mixture of individuals attending varied from young single working people, young couples with families, to middle aged couples and mature individuals with some investment background. Most of the attendees thought this was a novel plan and a different approach to wealth building, but had never been involved or even considered this approach as one that they would or could participate in. After much discussion, questions and presentations, someone did ask the question, "who's gonna watch the money?" Most of the attendees were thinking "what money – we have no money to watch." At the next meeting 18 persons showed up to help get the bus ("Vision") moving. Still nobody brought their $1000 – point is, make your initial investment or assessment realistic for the population you are investing with *(see chapter on "Lessons Learned")*. Although many may have had the $1000, some, of course, thought that was too much to invest in such a new concept. So the question is, "what would be a good initial startup for a group looking to increase their financial wherewithal?" The answer to that question is different from person to person and from investment group to investment group. With this investment concept being so new to many in this group, the investment amount was reduced to $600 annually or $50 per month. *"Little becomes much when you place it in the Master's hands!"* [2]

As in common with any new idea or venture, especially financial, everybody in attendance really wanted to participate. Yes, most liked the idea and the proposed outcome, but did not have the finances nor the courage to get on the bus for this financial, yet spiritual ride. Once all the questions and presentations had finally settled, then it was a matter of our group name for the core group of 18 members. However, over the next 6 years our core group dwindled down from 18 to a partnership of 8 due to changes in people's lives. Finally, we ended up with an all-important question, "what should we call ourselves?"

What's in a Name?

Every organization, business or investment group has or needs a name that identifies who they are and what they are doing. For this group various ideas for names were bantered about. Some of the suggested names were TP Network (The Positive Network), B.I.G. (Black Investment Group), Unique Enterprises and The Group. The majority voted on the name *Unique Enterprises*, chosen because this is a unique experience for individuals and families that make up this group. Our group now had a name and of course, having a catchy and befitting name was not enough.

"My mother always used to say, don't just sit around and complain about things, do something!"
Vice President, Kamala Harris

Chapter 2

<u>Where Do We Go From Here?</u>

Wealth building, whether it is mental, physical or financial can be a challenge for individuals, families, communities or even investment groups. However, it can be accomplished with time and education. Money minded and spiritually speaking, giving a percentage of your mind, money and muscles will reap untold benefits. With this in mind, the most important thing is to get started. Remember, even with research and life experiences, you will not know everything but you must start somewhere. So here is how we got started.

We began paying monthly dues in the amount of $35 that we later increased to $50 dollars. We want to say here that sometimes we need to take a step backward in order to go forward. With monthly dues we were able to begin to build our bank account; however, we quickly realized that we would have to increase our efforts if we were going to achieve our financial goals. This is how we entered into the world of creative fundraising.

An interesting and unique way we raised money and generated capital is to have a flea market because we found that "one man's trash is another man's treasure". Each partner went through their gently owned and used stuff and found items to contribute that were no longer beneficial to them. Our initial idea for raising funds using the flea market scenario was that we would utilize a space at one of the City's already existing flea markets taking the approach "why try to reinvent the wheel"? We saw many other people attending and selling things weekly, so this seemed like a great idea that would work perfectly for us. Let us say here, that there are some disadvantages to renting space at someone else's flea market. First of all, the space must be rented, one has to jockey for a good space which means getting there early. You have to hope for good weather (not too hot or too cold) and most of all, a crowd of interested and capable buyers. Even with all of this working in your favor, you still may go home with very few items sold and no funds raised (after the outgoing cost to secure the spot).

On a positive note, one of our club members cleaned out her closet with the foresight that women's shoes, handbags and accessories would do well. Of course, our member, being an avid shopper, needed to make room for more and more shoes, handbags and accessories in her closet. The process helped to foster team building amongst our membership which proved to be paramount in the weeks, months and years to come. There was a team assigned to dealing with the City to secure the space including needed permits, etc. A team was assigned to labeling and tagging the sale items. We took turns, in teams of twos, at manning our store for the day.

To avoid a lot of nonsense and in-house disagreements, (there no doubt will be some) it is imperative that the group know each other as best as you can know a business partner. In our group there are early risers, afternoon thinkers, salespersons, introverts, extroverts, frontliners, background workers and just plain talkers. We needed all of these to make the ship move smoothly. To get the maximum mileage from each business partner, each one must be placed where he or she can best "walk in his or her own lane".

Some of the other fundraising attempts (some very successful, some fairly successful and others mild disasters) included a barbeque delivery service for Friday and Saturday lunch, a sightseeing (wink, wink) bus trip to Reno, Nevada, a prayer breakfast, crab feed, a Black History Gospel fest, a candy sale, an investment on a "Gospel on the Green concert, and a penny drive following Oprah Winfrey's lead from her very popular and successful television show. We even partnered with a local restaurant chain that would assist in various groups' fundraising efforts. As you can imagine not everything we tried was a financial success, but the important thing is that we were not afraid to try. Some of our efforts cost us money and some of our efforts allowed the group to reap a harvest. One of the keys to a successful fundraiser is that you must think through your activity, with all members totally committed to the project. At the end of all of our various fundraising efforts, faithfully paying dues, and much prayer, we accumulated more than $10,000. We were now ready, or we thought we were ready to invest. Most of all, don't neglect to pray both individually and collectively that the chosen activity is in line with the group's overall mission.

By the way, speaking of a "mission statement", our group did not have a formal mission statement. The mission was always kind of "understood". It was never formalized on paper or for that matter even really discussed. All we knew was that we wanted to make some money. As we got further we realized that we needed to educate ourselves as much as we could. The mission statement would later become more defined and documented.

CHAPTER 3
Starting Our Organization

Entering into this venture, one of the things we had to decide was our structure. Do we want to be a partnership, or a limited liability corporation? We didn't know how to begin to draw up any kind of agreement, but we did know how to ask for help from an expert. Here are some of the tips or advice we were given by some of the professionals we looked to for advice and guidance:

First...Commitment

All members/partners MUST be totally committed if the Group is to work and survive. Believe us when we say that total commitment would be paramount more times than we ever thought. Do not go into ANY agreement with ANY person that is not committed with their time and finances. That can and will lead to problems later.

Second...Legal Structure

We made a list of all of the things we wanted or things that we thought we would like to see in the partnership/corporation agreement. We were cautioned not to leave any stones unturned, because this is a business and a legal document and whatever is in the agreement or

17

not in the agreement, will stand up in a court of law. We learned that In a corporation, any member or partner can sell their shares to anyone they choose and that person or persons will automatically become a part of our group. We were warned that in a partnership, a member's personal assets can become a target in case of a lawsuit. That was a startling concept to know that personal assets could become a target in case of a lawsuit if we became a partnership. Our founder/organizer and senior (by age) of the group thought "what a shame it would be or could be to work many, many years to accumulate personal assets and then lose it because of an error in judgment made by the group." How scary can that be? With much discussion the group decided to become a partnership. We went to the proper authority and got the paperwork needed such as a fictitious name statement. We then placed our ad in the newspaper as required, making our big announcement. After paying the required fees, we thought we had completed our goal. It was not long until we discovered that an attorney was needed to draw up the agreement and an accountant was needed to prepare financial statements. We also needed a financial institution to establish a banking relationship for future endeavors. **Warning;** The search for a financial institution that was willing to work with a new venture was no picnic in any sense of the word. We discovered that banks needed and required even more paperwork than the State and County. Fortunately for us, we spoke to someone that worked in the banking industry, and she was happy to help and guide us in getting the needed paperwork to present to a financial institution. (It is always great to know someone that knows someone that knows someone). Needless to say we were able to work with that bank for many years.

PEOPLE NEED PEOPLE

All business ventures need people to make a successful business. We would like to share some tips and suggestions that we had to consider and found beneficial in getting this venture under way. Understand that an investment group will only be as good as the people that come to the table. We looked for people with characteristics and talents that we thought we would have synergy with. We needed people that we felt could be faithful in good times and bad times. There will be ups and downs and personalities are bound to clash. We discovered we needed people with different viewpoints that would not be afraid to challenge the group in a businesslike and professional way. We wanted people who were willing to take some time and energy devoted to learning including reading books and attending seminars is truly a must for this group.

Every organization must have at least one or two risk-takers or wild cards as we called them. It is important that you identify your wild cards and risk takers. Do not make the mistake or mistakes of sweeping their suggestions of seemingly risky ventures under the rug. Believe it or not our most successful venture financially, out of all of our ventures we've considered, was presented to the group by one of our risk taker wildcards. We decided to take the risk and jump in with both feet. Do not count these folks out! You may want to identify them by other names i.e. "Out of the box thinkers", "overzealous", "over excited", and just "weird thinkers". On the flip side you will also need some conservatives in the group to bring the "voice of reason". You can't play longshots all the time. Wealth is a slow steady process. While the high return on investment (R.O.I.) may be attractive on a gamble, the slow and steady return on a secure play is sometimes the way to go. Bottom line is the makeup of your group should be as diverse as your future investments. Remember that all opinions matter. The aggressive risk taker, the middle of the road thinker and the conservative mindset all bring value and have opinions that must be considered.

A Concrete Plan

Once the membership was in place, we ascertained that our plan had to be concrete. A plan that can be articulated with clarity and simplicity to any future partners and prospects is something we worked on in depth. We knew our plan MUST be accompanied with a strong passion for success. If there is no passion for the Plan, it will come through loud and clear. We attempted to make our plan a "gut" thing to go along with a "head and heart" thing. Once we had interested parties, we took a strong look at what they could bring and/or were willing to bring to the table. We were determined not to go into the plan with the idea that we must accept any and all that showed an interest in becoming a part of our group. One of our most interesting prospects wanted to be sure that our partnership agreement included a "do not touch another partner's spouse or significant other" clause. Needless to say the agreement did not and does not include that clause; however, to this day it does bring a smile and a good laugh to the group. We needed to know what we were looking for and go after those persons that would be an asset to the membership. Now this is not to say that individuals that you may think of as not suitable for the Plan cannot be nurtured to bring out hidden talents.

Since this was a new concept to us, we knew little about what to expect. Enthusiastically we sought out how to make the venture a success by studying other investment clubs' operations. We were not interested in the business of reinventing the wheel. We knew we could learn from other prospering business' stories and methods and make them our own.

We would like to share some of the many resources and/or books that impacted us in the beginning of this organization and we would like to share a few things from some of the partners that we think will be of interest to you.

First Home Purchase - Madeline

I was inspired by the pamphlet "Jessica Rent-No-More" that was shared at one of our meetings by a partner. It listed the benefits of homeownership and outlined the process of purchasing a home. At the time my husband and I were renters. My entire family were homeowners, so I understood the importance and pride of having a home. However, there was the enormous financial responsibility of owning a house that was extremely frightening to me. My husband and I were just starting out and I wasn't ready to take on such an adult responsibility yet. So many questions swirled in my head of what could happen if we weren't able to keep up with our payments. Also, I had finally started to save and accumulate a nice nest egg in my first IRA at work and I didn't want it to disappear. There was also the fear that we would be denied a loan by banks and I didn't want to go through that humiliation.

However, I had a young son to consider and wanted him to grow up in a home of his own. My reservations of taking money out of my IRA for a down payment were legitimate, but my friend and partner Lynee reminded me of the bigger picture of investment and growth in value from equity. She herself had just purchased her first home, a condo, and had had the same reservations as myself so she completely understood. We moved out of our apartment after our rent was increased a third time and into my mom's house to save money. My husband and I went forward with the pre-qualification and pre-approval process and then had to figure out what type of property we wanted to purchase as first-time homeowners. We preferred starting off small, with a townhouse or condo, but God had other plans and we were blessed with an exquisite single-family home within our budget. Within the same year our family grew as we were blessed with our beautiful daughter Elianna. God is good!

Investment Lessons - Keith

"The Beardstown Ladies" Investment book was another resource we used that made a positive impact for our group. We studied the book together and learned the ins and outs of investing in stocks including lessons in setting up an investment club, picking stocks, selling and buying stocks, reading and understanding annual reports, and choosing the right brokerage company to work with your organization. It was inspiring for us to see senior citizens be so successful in the stock market and gave us hope that we could be just as successful. At each meeting I would lead the group and we would be given homework assignments to read for the next meeting. One of our assignments was to choose a stock and explain why we chose it. Madeline chose Chiron because it was a pharmaceutical company near her job and she heard they were working on some new drugs. We charted all the members' chosen stocks and followed them for a year to see where their value would end up. To Madeline's surprise and delight, her Chiron stock earned the most value for the year.

During our early years we had many speakers to come and share their knowledge with us to form stepping stones on our bridge from ignorant to the beginnings journey of opportunity. We heard from a bank professional that discussed the 4C's of Lending; Character, Credit Worthiness, Capital and Collateral. A real estate agent discussing equity sharing and how to get financing, a real estate broker educated on the difference between prequalifying for a loan and being pre-approved. Another real estate investor shared how to leverage your money in real estate as well as working within a partnership as opposed to investing on your own. An attorney came in to talk about legal documents required for starting an organization (LLC vs partnership and a corporation vs sole proprietorship). Lastly, we learned about 1031 Exchanges that allows owners to forego capital gains.

Time to get started

At this time, we felt that we had invested in and taken our time to get some studies done, and some education under our belts (as you will see in our education chapter). We were now ready to buckle down, get this party started and jump into the PROCESS.

"If opportunity doesn't knock, build a door"

Affirmation

CHAPTER 4

The Process

Opportunity sometimes comes knocking at your door at unexpected times and in unexpected ways. It is in these moments that you just have to take a leap of faith into unknown territory and believe in the process.

In 1997, the board members of a non-profit housing development corporation, decided at their board meeting that they were not interested in developing the 55th Street project. One of the partners of Unique, William Randolph, was doing a job there and overheard the conversation and brought it to the group. Could it be he just happened to be in the right place and time and knew this was a golden opportunity for Unique?

In February 1998, the "Wild Card" partner of our group excitedly called a special meeting of the members and we came together to discuss the possible real estate deal, the way we usually do. After we heard the proposition and proposal to purchase this property and had been given as much information as we could process at the time, we decided to look into this project more closely. However, some members were reluctant to the idea of purchasing a lot in Oakland. This was not the kind of project we had planned on starting out with because we had never built anything before. Honestly, it seemed to be an unbelievable and overwhelming endeavor to the group. For one thing, we didn't have a lot of money at the time and we didn't have credit worthiness as an investment club. We went back and forth about the pros and cons of moving forward with the opportunity and the potential risks involved. However, with still a bit of concern, we all hesitantly got on board with the project's process. The group discussed the options of what to do with the lot in case we were successful with the purchase. Our options were buying and selling it as a flip to make a profit to build up our credit-worthiness as a group or develop it into a residential dwelling. In retrospect, building a multi unit residence, four-plex, duplex, home or even a small house from the ground up was never something we really thought we wanted to do, but we eventually did just that!

The process was set in motion as William set-up a meeting with the owner of the property to discuss the terms of purchasing the lot. The owner of the lot originally wanted $50,000 for the lot but he said he would consider negotiating the cost. However, the owner wanted it to be purely a cash deal. Since Unique did not have $50,000 just laying around to purchase anything, we offered him $25,000 with 10% down and a closing escrow in 45 days. The owner countered with $35,000 and we agreed with a 45-day close. We agreed to the owner's counteroffer but unfortunately that amount was only for the cost of the lot. We still needed a loan to complete the purchase. As a group we had to figure out where these funds were going to come from. A committee was sent out to meet with a financial advisor about financing for our "window of opportunity". Mary & William met with a local mortgage broker and discovered that Unique Enterprises as a new entity was not credit worthy to obtain a loan on its own merit, therefore we needed a "front-person" to qualify for the loan. Again, we are not suggesting that this is the best route for another group and there were times we felt that this advice was not good for us either. We now had a contract to purchase the lot with a 45-day closing but not enough capital to complete the deal. Since the lot already had cement stairs on it, we found out that we could qualify for rehabilitation funding in addition to the remainder of the purchase price of the lot plus funds for construction.

The lot was 3,955 square feet and zoned for a single-family dwelling located in Oakland, California. We obtained building plans to construct a duplex but it turned out that the lot was 45 square feet short of the legal limit that the City normally allows for a multiple-unit building The lot needed to be 4,000 square feet. We were told that we could apply for and obtain a variance so that we could proceed with construction. Of course, being new to the game of real estate ventures we had no idea what a variance was or the process to obtain the needed variance, but we sure did learn fast. We were informed that we had to get a permit from the City of Oakland to build on this specific plot of land deemed short of the legal limit. In this process, the surrounding neighborhood residents had to be notified and a meeting was scheduled to hear the plans and voice any concerns that they may have. At the City meeting our variance was approved almost unanimously, save one vote.

The biggest question became "how were we going to finance this project?" However, we took this process seriously and looked at each member's credit status to locate the front person. The creditworthiness of many of our members wasn't that great, but we took a chance on one member and vice versa. He was approved for the loan, much to his absolute shock. Surprise, surprise, surprise!! We found our front person and he was even amazed at how good he looked on paper. This is a great example of what a committed member of the group will do for the sake of all members. Even though he and his wife were in the process of purchasing a home of their own, they had noreservations to get this done for the group. We were able to obtain a lender for our project with a residential construction loan. The funds were released based on our contractor's completion of phases in building the property.

Simultaneously, we realized we needed a land surveyor and architectural plans to move forward with our intentions to develop the land. Fortunately, the person living next door to the property was an architect that drew the plans for his own property, so we entered into a contract with him to draw up similar plans for our property. In hindsight and in our anxiousness to get the process moving, we neglected to do our due diligence; therefore, we originally paid too much for the plans. However, after doing some research, we received a partial refund for the land survey and architectural plans. We also found that the lot was not completely vacant and was quite a blight to the neighborhood. It was an overgrown, unkempt community garden that was hiding many things including carrots, tree stumps, cement stairs, neighborhood trash, a pipe for a gas line and "Mary Jane" that had to be cleared away.

In addition to that, there was a list of other things we needed to do such as taking our survey and plans to the City's Planning Department where they review your building concept and approve it. As we stated earlier, the lot was too small for our architectural plans and the variance needed to be reviewed by the Planning Commission. Upon the approval of plans, we then had to go to the Building department to get a building permit at an initial cost of $3,500. Additionally, we learned of other fees unknown to us such as school tax, bedroom tax and that electrical, plumbing & HVAC (heating, ventilation and air conditioning) was part of the building permit.

In the process Unique as an organization had desired to employ individuals and minority-owned businesses to help accomplish our development dreams. We had already overcome some major hurdles, so with our building permit in hand, it was now time to choose a contractor. One thing we want to mention is that this process could have gone so much smoother for us had we done our due diligence and not depended so much on those we thought were knowledgeable of the process. In hindsight, which is always

20/20, we should have had the building permits obtained from the City by the General Contractor, if we had one, instead of doing it ourselves. Oh well! That, and many more hard lessons were soon to be learned.

We looked at a number of contractors from references and referrals obtained from others. Unfortunately, the contractor of choice, which was most reasonable, was unavailable (they had taken a $2 million job in San Francisco, CA), so we turned to another contractor who assured us that they could and would do the job well; however, their price would be $10,000 more than our contractor of choice. Much to our dismay the company we contracted with, that we thought was a qualified general contractor, was, in actuality, only a framing contractor. All we were left with was the framing of one floor of a two-story structure and costly timber left on the project site to warp in the winter weather. This was the beginning of our education with contractors. In hind-sight, make sure your written construction contract is tight.

So, we picked ourselves up, picked up our wood and hired what we thought was a real general contractor for this project. As fate would have it, this supposed general contractor was really just a roofer with bogus credentials. To

33

make matters worse when our new contractor approached the City to inform them that they would now be the contractor on record, we were informed that our building permits had expired and would cost additional money to reinstate! We were facing yet another financial set-back, but with God's help we somehow found the funds needed to overcome it. After the contractor straightened out the warped wood, framed the second story of our project and constructed the roof, we had to sever that relationship as well.

We had yet another mind-blowing occurrence regarding the electrical work for the house which taught us a very valuable lesson. Never cut corners in the foundational elements of building a house. We hired an electrician to come in, but he was only an apprentice. We were looking to do things inexpensively and stretch our funds. He said he could do the work and save us money. Regrettably, his work didn't pass the inspection and it cost us even more money. The walls had to be re-opened and all the wiring completely replaced.

In frustration and absolute disgust, one of our members inquired of a member of his family about the electrician they had recently hired to do work on their home. They were very pleased with his work, so he contacted him and asked him to look at the electrical work that was done.

He came to look at the property and gave us an estimate of the cost for his work. In the end, we finally ended up with an A+ contractor who not only did the work correctly, but did it in a timely manner for us to move forward.

Now as for the completion of this project, this is how things unfolded; After the dismissal of the first two "contractors" believe it or not there were two others. Our choices of contractors seem to have gotten worse instead of better. We were paying out thousands of dollars and getting hundreds of dollars worth of work. By this time most of us were tired, weary, worn, frustrated and some of us were just downright angry we had dealt with so many unscrupulous and unprofessional so-called contractors.

In desperation one of our members, Jamal, reached out to an old high school classmate, who was in the home improvement field. He came to the project site to take a look at the building's condition. He immediately made suggestions and assisted us in the finishing of the interior structure of the building. Keith and Jamal took his instructions and began working at putting in cabinets, sinks, toilets, and all fixtures within the building. They also worked on putting up sheetrock and the cutting and installing baseboards. His friend's help and follow through was truly a blessing for Unique at a time when we needed it most.

At this time, our construction funds were almost exhausted and we knew that we had to pull it together among ourselves and put in sweat equity to finish the project. Most importantly, we needed more money to complete the project. God sent us a miracle by allowing us to refinance our construction loan when the property was still in the construction phase, into a conventional loan. After the loan was approved and funded, we learned that typically a property is not eligible to qualify for a conventional loan until after the structure is completed and the Certificate of Occupancy has been issued. This meant we were moved out of the higher interest construction loan and into a lower rate conventional loan. Wow! Glory to God! Our new mortgage broker, whom Jamal met through divine circumstance, said to him after our loan was approved. "I don't know what deity you pray to but continue to pray to and praise him! In all my years of doing this, I've never seen a loan get approved in this scenario where the structure is not 100% completed."

Even though we now had more funds to press on, eventually it became evident that we had gotten to a point where we needed more help. Meredith, one of our members, had a friend with a crew. She asked if any of the crew members could assist us. We got two guys who were finishers, to basically work on putting up the sheetrock and joint compound during the day. They did such a phenomenal job completing that task that we had them assist us with additional tasks to expedite the project. Because of our previous experiences with so-called professionals, we became our own contractors. Keep in mind that all of the partners had full time jobs, businesses to run and families to attend to. However, each day after work we all convened at the site to finish and complete the building. We worked tirelessly for months each night and even weekends installing door stops, closet doors, painting and making corrections to sheetrock along with other things to get things ready for the final inspection.

On the day of the final inspection, we were praying and holding our breaths. Our greatest hope was that the inspector would finally approve and sign off that the 55th Street Project. The inspector looked around and made some suggestions, inciteful comments and we started to fear that this meant he would not sign off on the building. However, to our utter amazement and relief, he did just that. **We were finally approved**! It was time to celebrate our journey together and bask in the joy of what we had accomplished in building our beautiful duplex! What a glorious day it was when the final inspection was done and we received the precious golden "Certificate of Occupancy".

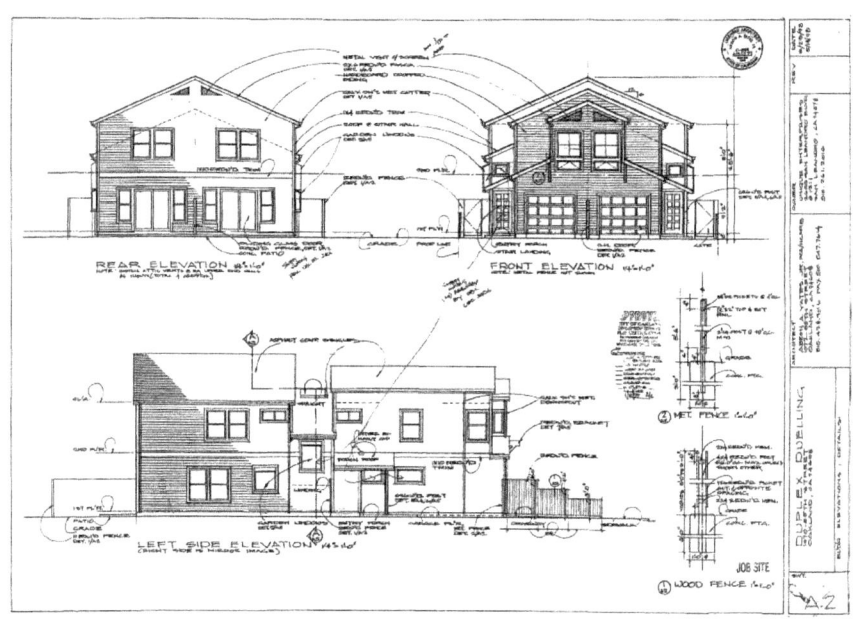

`Architectural plans
rear, front and side elevations*

38

First floor framing

Front elevation almost completed

Our completed 1st project

"Hold fast to dreams, for if dreams die, life is a broken-winged bird that cannot fly"

Langston Hughes

Chapter 5
<u>Lessons Learned</u>

Looking back at what it took to come together as a unified group; the process of raising capital, deciding on how to best use said capital when the options seem limitless, and all the steps and processes in between and after in the construction of our first building, you can best believe that there were a multitude of lessons learned.

Keep in mind that none of us in this partnership had ever done anything like this before. While we all have varied backgrounds and expertise, we realized and learned quickly that to get to where we wanted to go, we would have to lean on each other and unless we intended on doing everything by ourselves, we needed help. I would say that our first, most important and often our most expensive lessons centered around one unpredictable commodity; PEOPLE.

When our founder put the word out to put a group like this together, school was in session and the lessons began.

PEOPLE LESSON ONE:
"Work With the Willing"

There were over twenty people at our first organizational meeting. Out of that twenty or so that came to hear about the idea of coming together, ten to twelve were excited about going ahead with the idea. Soon thereafter, though, we dwindled down to our core of eight.

While we wanted all of our friends and loved ones to join us in this endeavor, not everyone had the foresight, vision, time or wherewithal to take the action necessary to participate in this venture.

PEOPLE LESSON TWO:
"Trustworthiness Over Talent"

We started by looking internally at our circle of influence. It is in this sphere that you may find your greatest assets. Our group has some talented people in it. We have an insurance professional, an engineer, an I.T. professional, a hotel executive and a worker in the school system to name some of the professions. More importantly, all members are people of integrity. When you are talking about entering into ventures of 4, 5, and potentially 6-figures, you MUST have people who are trustworthy in all circumstances. You need people who are risk takers and investors. People who are willing to commit to the financial obligation of startup capital and continuous financial responsibilities you may face as a group.

Most of all, surround yourself with people who are not quitters and who will always have your back no matter the costs. We found out what Unique was made of as members when we did not turn on each other even in the darkest of days. What we learned beyond a shadow of doubt is our group could go through the fire together.

PEOPLE LESSON THREE:
"Have patience and work your plan"

Have a concrete written plan which can be referred to when times get rough and memory fades. A plan that can be articulated with clarity and simplicity to any future partners and prospects is a must. The plan must be accompanied with a strong passion. Once you have interested parties in your plan, you should take a strong look at what they can bring and/or willing to bring to the table. Many times it is good to follow your instincts and do your research so you will be clear about what your needs are. As with any good plan, always PLAN - DO - REVIEW. Don't hesitate to make changes when needed.

In the process of building our duplex we had many interactions with government agencies where we learned the lesson of patience. We learned that the inner workings of our City were convoluted and confusing, often sending us in circles or on wild goose chases in the permit or inspection process. One person would give us one story while another would give us completely different information.

We also experienced the same misinformation from our many contractors. After a while we thought dealing with contractors just seemed like a legal way to steal. Despite several false starts and frustration, we prayed, persevered and forged ahead.

Once our building was completed, we entered into the wonderful world of property management. Again, patience was a virtue well learned as we dealt with lease agreements, screening of potential renters, credit reports, and Section 8 requirements for rentals in our city. We learned the differences between what a good tenant versus a bad tenant looked like very quickly which led to another lesson of how best and legally to rid ourselves of that tenant in an expedient manner through the eviction process.

PEOPLE LESSON FOUR:
"Don't misplace your trust"

Although we trusted each other, we extended that trust to everyone outside our group to a fault. We have been burned by people that have shown themselves to be untrustworthy. We have had some expensive lessons for our naivete. When you have a group of honest people you just think that other "professionals" will be honest in their dealings with you. Ask for, then check the references to find people that you are reasonably convinced will catch the vision and work the plan. DO YOUR DUE DILIGENCE.

PEOPLE LESSON FIVE:

"Hire slowly but fire quickly"

At the beginning, one of the most exciting parts of building was the prospect of employing others while we grew. We hired and helped several people, many we knew but some we didn't, both of which presented challenges as we progressed. A basic rookie mistake we made was not checking references before jumping in. Once problems began, we extended time, gave more additional time, swallowed excuses and endeavored to treat everyone more than fair even as our confidence level dwindled. Eventually, we owned our mistakes and regretfully severed business relationships that did not meet our needs or honor their contract. In hindsight, spending whatever time you have to in order to do a thorough vetting is worth the time, energy and money. As soon as a contract is out of compliance, ACT - don't delay.

"Change will not come if we wait for some other person or some other time. We are the ones we've been waiting for. We are the change that we seek."
Barack Obama, 44th President of the United States

Chapter 6
<u>EDUCATION</u>

__Education__.........The act or process of imparting or acquiring general knowledge, developing the powers of reasoning and judgment, and generally of preparing oneself or others intellectually for mature life. __Instruction__, development of knowledge. The means through which the aims and habits of a group of people lives on from one generation to the next as defined by Webster. Education is learning, instructing and imparting knowledge.

What do you do when you don't know what to do? In our case we recognized first that we didn't know enough to move forward. After that, we utilized our internal resources to help us learn about different areas of investing. Note: Whatever you do, don't talk to anyone who is not knowledgeable in what they're talking about. Invite those with a specific area of expertise to speak to your group. There are many experts willing and waiting to pass on information to those willing to listen!

Education was key in the commencement of our group. We looked into various ways of educating ourselves. We weren't quite sure which direction we wanted to invest in so we inquired and researched different modes of investment opportunities. We began our educational quest by reading newspapers and magazine articles on areas of interest. One of the partners brought one of our first book reads to the group, "The Beardstown Ladies Common Sense Investment Guide" [3]. It helped direct us into the wonderful world of investing. Keith took the reins and led us in the study. We spent many meeting hours analyzing their ideas and experiences which even provided the seed of the idea to write this book! We used this book to get our feet wet in the marvelous world of stock investment. We didn't have a clue where to start, so we thought reading and investigating the path of a group of successful senior ladies wouldn't be a bad choice unlike today where information is readily available at your fingertips on any subject matter. After all, if they could be successful then so could we. At the time, the book was one of the media darlings for investing that could be understood by any layperson. Each chapter was full of ideas of how to start an investment club and learn about the intricacies of the stock market. We thought the book would be a great model upon which we could build our investment club. Each week Keith gave us reading assignments and at the following meetings, we would discuss our findings and the knowledge we acquired. It was fascinating learning a whole new language of the stock market. Our group found the book easy to follow because it wasn't full of technical terms that was above our heads. The subject matter was written in a way that we could bite into each digestible morsel of information. We learned where and how to choose a stock of interest and even had an assignment to choose a stock and follow it. Each of us chose stocks that were of interest to us based on the industry we were currently working in. Some of the stocks we followed ranged from the hotel industry to health industry to the toy industry. In the end, Madeline's Chiron stock outperformed all the rest. It was a very proud moment for her.

We decided that for now, stock would be our main focus. We purchased various stocks with one example being "On Sale" @ $6.00 per share. We watched that stock along with others, rise to over $90.00 per share. We sold our position at over $70.00 per share which gave us enough money to proceed with our other investment opportunities. Sometime later, we found out that there were discrepancies between what "The Beardstown Ladies" had written and their actual return on their stocks but by then we were on our way and moved on to other influences. Once the mind expands it can never go back so thank you for opening up that path Beardstown ladies!

We were constantly looking out for newspaper articles to share with the group. The power of knowledge was growing rapidly in our unit. Just taking the time to scan the paper, check the internet and tune our ears into our surroundings each day gave us great insight and money saving tips we could use personally, as well as educate our families and friends. We read articles about how to get a good used car, knowing the differences between a Trust, Living Will and Ordinary Will, how to retrieve unclaimed property and not being taken advantage of by your bank. There are even articles about good stress versus bad stress that we could learn from. One particular pamphlet called "Jessica Rent No More" was the catalyst of change in our group because it led us all to obtaining the "American Dream" of becoming homeowners. Of course, before we could even think about purchasing property, we needed to find out how to get the bank loan.

One of our amazing guest speakers was a mortgage broker who came to our group and educated us on the nuances of pre-qualification and pre-approval. The bottom line is that you should be prepared! We found that it's better to do both before venturing out to look at homes that may be way out of your range. Getting pre-qualified is the initial step in the mortgage process. And it's generally fairly simple. You supply a bank or lender with your overall financial picture, including your debt, income and assets. After evaluating this information, a lender can give you an idea of the mortgage amount for which you can qualify. Pre-Approval was the next step in the process. Complete an official mortgage application (and usually pay an application fee) then supply the lender with the necessary documentation to perform an extensive check on your financial background and current credit rating to figure out what mortgage amount you'd be approved for.

We could never have imagined that we would learn as much as we have. The wealth of information that this group has been privy to is unbelievable. It has been said, "Get all you can and can all you get". Truly "applied" knowledge is power but with that knowledge comes responsibility and we believe we have all become a little bit more responsible with our gifts, talents and treasures.

In addition to becoming students in the business world, we also wanted to become students spiritually. We wanted to do business by the Good Book! Therefore our meetings included lessons from the Holy Bible (which continues to this day). We found that a spiritual belief for us was helpful and kept the group centered and grounded. We are not saying a spiritual belief is a must to do business, because we have seen, read about and know of many successful businessmen and women not claiming any spiritual belief. However, for us it was and is essential to rely on our faith. Some of the topics we looked at included:

- The fruitlessness of worrying
- Giving God time to work

- Gossiping and slandering (the dangers)
- Love
- Faith and Action
- The loyalty of followship
- Sharing blessings with others

We wanted you to know how we went about educating ourselves. You may find that some of what we used may not be right for you and your group. Some of the information may be outdated but the concepts will never change.

Sharing blessings with others is another lesson that we have taken seriously, and that we have built our group around. The bible says "but I say, he which soweth sparingly shall also reap sparingly; and he which soweth bountifully, shall reap also bountifully" (2 Corinthians 9:6 KJV). This lesson taught us the importance of giving freely to each other and giving cheerfully outside the group. Of course we are not speaking strictly monetarily; however, we have sown and reaped our share of that also. We strive to never miss an opportunity to share memorable occasions with others whether it is during a stressful time of bereavement, a joyful time in the birth of a new baby, a new home, a graduation or two lives joined together in marriage. Sharing blessings for us is paramount and we are so blessed to have taken a part in each other's lives in the purchases of new homes, graduations and milestones of our children and birthday celebrations.

In one of our lessons, we looked at the "sense of a goose" and discovered that if we had the sense of a goose, we would stand by each other when things got tough. When the lead goose gets tired, he moves back and allows another goose to take the lead. The application of that story has worked for us many, many times and we want to share it with you now.

THE SENSE OF A GOOSE

In the fall when you see geese heading south for the winter flying along in "V" formation, you might be interested in knowing what science has discovered about why they fly that way.

It has been learned that as each bird flaps its wings, it creates an uplift for the bird immediately following. By flying in a "V" formation, the whole flock adds at least 71 percent greater flying range than if each bird flew on its own.

People who share a common direction and sense of community can get where they are going quicker and easier, because they are traveling on the thrust of one another.

Whenever a goose falls out of formation, it suddenly feels the drag and resistance of trying to go it alone, and quickly gets back into formation to take advantage of the lifting power of the bird immediately in front.

If we had as much sense as a goose, we will stay in formation with those who are headed in the same way we are going.

When the lead goose gets tired, he rotates back in the wing and another goose flies point.

It pays to take turns doing hard jobs with people or with geese flying south.

The geese honk from behind to encourage those up front to keep up their speed.

What messages do we give when we honk from behind?

Finally, when a goose gets sick or is wounded by gunshot and falls out, two geese fall out of formation and follow him down to help and protect him. They stay with him until he is either able to fly or until he is dead, and then they launch out on their own or with another formation to catch up with their group.

If we had the sense of a goose, we would stand by each other like that. [4]

Chapter 7
Sell the Building

After four long and frustrating years, in what we thought would take 6 to 9 months, the project was finally complete. Renters were in place and minor repairs and finishing touches were being made. Behind us was the search for competent contractors. In the past were the days of faxes and emails for draw requests from our financer to pay for laborers and materials that at times didn't seem to be advancing our cause. Behind us was the incident of having to tear out the electrical wiring, because we hired an apprentice and not a licensed electrician, in our attempt to save some money. That was an expensive lesson. In our rear-view mirror were the challenges of hiring contractor after contractor after contractor that made us various promises but never delivered. Over were the tense (to put it politely) meetings we had when it came time to pay the mortgage on a building we were not yet making any money on. Over and done with were the times spent working well into the evenings after working an 8 hour day on our "regular jobs". Best of all, we no longer had to explain to Mary or Jamal why this wasn't done or that wasn't completed and when will we get our "Certificate of Occupancy" so we can put a bow on this project.

The day we passed our final inspection and received our Certificate Of Occupancy was an amazing, joyful, "Hallelujah, thank you JESUS!!!" moment in the life of our organization. All of our sacrifices were FINALLY going to start paying dividends. So, what now? Do we immediately put this on the market and sell it to recoup our investment and walk away with a little profit, or should we be landlords for a while and get a monthly income and sell later? Well, we felt that after the four L-O-O-N-N-G-G years it took to get us to this point, we should let this investment pay us for a while. That means we needed tenants to occupy our newly created domicile. The problem was none of us were ever landlords before. I (the writer of this chapter) thought to myself, "How hard can it be. I mean, just slap a "For Rent" sign on it, select someone and start collecting rents." If I had it to do over again, I would definitely recommend using a Property Manager. For what they cost, they save you a lot of headache. We didn't use one so we had to personally set the rental price. As an organization we did not want to take advantage of any tenant by asking for rents that would be a hardship for anyone. We believe it was our mission to take this opportunity to provide a quality residence at an affordable monthly rate, but at the same time receiving a positive cash flow to recoup some of our expenditures. We had to ask ourselves, "Is the rent too high? Is it too low? What are other places in the market renting for?" We decided to do our own promotion to get potential applicants. Then after receiving applications and weeding through them, we interviewed and chose our prospective tenants.

We were about a year and a half to two years into our role as landlords when we, as an organization, found out the tough way that the plan you start with may have to be altered to fit God's plans. Understand that the goals and/or ideas that you start out with sometimes do not go as intended. The original plan going into this was to purchase a lot, construct a building and sell it for a profit. Just like it was Moses' plan to spend the rest of his life in Midian tending Jethro's sheep, it was never our intention or purpose to become landlords. With all the out-of-pocket expenses and credit card debts we incurred to get this project complete, it was the feeling of the group that we could recoup some of our money with the positive cash flow of the monthly rents we were receiving. After all of our sweat equity, we fell in love with our finished building and could not bear the thought of parting with "our baby". We became attached to wood, stucco and window panes. However, we could not ignore the behavior of the Bay Area housing market at this time in the early 2000's. Properties that were once selling and renting for one price a few years prior were now going for double and sometimes triple of their former value. On a side note, don't ever forget to be flexible and willing to change your course when things do not go as planned or when God has a different course in mind. "His ways are not our ways and His thoughts are not our thoughts."

The lesson we learned was "never say never".

In business many times the "T" in "timing" is bigger than the "T" in "talent".

While we loved the positive monthly cash flow and the idea of having a six-figure asset on our books, we had many things that were at play that forced us to take some steps back and really look at "our baby" (the building) and the big picture objectively:

- The incredible appreciation of the Bay Area Housing Market
- The eviction of a difficult tenant at the time and having to deal with future tenants.
- The idea of "cashing out" and moving on to something else.

"Sell the building" had long been the mantra of one of our partners. The idea seemed to be gaining momentum as each week and month went by. Our maintenance team and one of the partners in particular had been working overtime (in addition to her regular 9 to 5) on tenant issues. She expressed some of the challenges and frustrations of maintaining a property. With hindsight being 20/20, again I would say that we would definitely hire a property manager if we could do it over again. All of the partners had full time careers and families to take care of as well. I don't think we fully anticipated all that went into property management. Advertising vacancies, receiving and reviewing applications, interviewing and screening tenants, building repairs all go into managing a property. To have that burden lifted off of us so we could focus on our monthly income would have been worth it to us.

We had a round table discussion regarding the merits of selling the building (or not). Each of us chimed in and gave our thoughts on whether to sell or hold. We were not all in agreement but the majority decision was to sell and reinvest the proceeds. We examined our goals, discussed that we must have something definite in mind for the proceeds from the sale. We did not want the funds to sit in a financial institution and slowly melt away and not have any assets to show or real estate in our portfolio at the end of the transaction. Selling the property would only be feasible if we were able to show a profit after all of our bills had been paid.

For starters we paid back the outside loans we incurred in addition to Unique's internal debts and finally the mortgage and the costs associated with selling the property. A Committee was formed to do research on the cost that would be associated with the transaction, and to find a suitable real estate broker to fit our situation. A special meeting was called for the sole purpose of discussing the committee's findings. The chairperson gave a complete analysis on the potential costs associated with the sale, and it was reported that we could make a handsome profit. Oh, how exciting that news was to hear! The two large variables would be the commission to the real estate broker and the planning ahead for the capital gains expense.

We are not advocating that this is right for everyone, but after much discussion it was decided that we would go with a broker who charged a flat fee instead of the standard 6% that most realtors charge. We felt that this particular realtor had the professionalism and competence to get the job done. However, there were still three key questions from our standpoint that needed to be answered:

- What would be the brokers' marketing plan for the property?
- Would there be any hidden additional fees not included in the proposal?
- What happens after the 90 days with no sale?

The broker we selected aggressively marketed our property, and the property was barely on the market for a month when we had an interested buyer. However, before we could close the deal on the sale, we had one final hurdle to clear. There was one last repair that needed to be completed before the deal was done. One of the partners had to go (after work) for a week and repair a damaged wall by one of our tenants. There turned out to be no hidden fees and the 90-day question became moot.

With the close of the escrow and the sale finally complete, our organization was sitting on over a half million dollars in funds! The feeling was truly exhilarating. We look back at the four long years of frustration prior to the close of this transaction and thank God for leading us. To be where we were at that moment, looking back at the overgrown weed-infested blight that we purchased, and to turn it into a completed two-story duplex worth over half a million dollars was nothing but an act of God. Seven of the eight of us had no experience whatsoever in this kind of venture. Lord knows we took our lumps, but through it all with prayer, patience, and persistence, we not only profited materially but also learned some valuable life lessons.

The evening of the next organizational meeting after the closing was an exciting time. Each member received a check paying them back for what they spent in the construction of our project plus a "little something" for their trouble. Most exciting was the realization that we could finally look forward to making plans on how to best put our proceeds to work. We gave thanks and praise to God because there were times when we really didn't know if, when or how we were going to get this done, so we always acknowledge HIM from whom all blessings flow. The sense of relief was un-measurable. Many of the real estate professionals that saw what we were trying to do, didn't give us much of a chance at pulling this off. I've heard many stories of people that have gone bankrupt in trying to do what we just managed to achieve. There was a great sense of relief, pride and accomplishment that we all felt when we had that check from the title company in our possession. And our friendships are still intact! Even now, we are amazed.

This whole ordeal gave us all encouragement to proceed fearlessly in other endeavors no matter what the naysayers may think. We know whose we are and the "Power of 8" is undeniable. A great leadership mentor, has a saying: "It's impossible to stop a man or woman who will not quit". How right that is.

Chapter 8

I Remember…

<u>The Good, The Bad, The Ugly</u>

When the sale of "our baby" was about to come to a close, the partners came together to discuss the possibility and probability of writing this book. All of the partners thought the world should hear and know our story because wisdom and blessings are to be shared not hoarded. In this chapter, we wanted to revisit the good, the bad and the ugly. Each partner had different recollections and thoughts of our journey. Here are a few memories that some of the partners would like to share with you.

<u>*Madeline- The Faithful Scribe*</u>

I remember the summer afternoon I drove by "The Lot" to take a second look at what I had just gotten myself into. At that time, the lot was less than (five) 5 minutes away from my job so I left work and found myself driving down 55th Street to take a gander. I stepped out of my car with my heart pumping and stood in front of a large filthy lot. I took a deep breath and then another. It was not the pristine, well-kept 3,955 square foot lot of land that I had anticipated seeing. Instead, there was a jungle of tall dense weeds the height of my hip or higher and debris covering the entire lot. Who knew what secrets, mysteries or dangers lay in those thick dark weeds. It was fenced off but seemed to be found as a personal dumping ground. It suddenly dawned on me that I was now part owner of this piece of land. Try as I might, I could not for the life of me, envision a duplex structure on this lot. "How in the world are we going to do this"? I thought. We are way in over our heads. {Can I please have a do-over Lord?} I was in my second trimester of pregnancy with our first child during that time so my hormones and emotions were at an all time high. My mind was racing with all the things that could possibly go wrong. All I could think about was how this venture would affect me and the future of my unborn child. I slowly raised my left hand to my swollen" bump" and prayed.

As the project progressed there came a day each partner was informed that we would have to pay $101.63 per member on the 55th Street mortgage. This made my heart sink precariously into my stomach. With my husband and I both partners of Unique, that came to a whopping $203.00 per month from our fragile budget. What I didn't know was within a few months we would each have to pony up a staggering $290.00 per partner!!! With a growing family, a mortgage of our own and other financial responsibilities, I felt like my worst nightmare had just come to life. It was only by the grace of God and "creative financing" that we were able to come up with the funds each month. We had much sacrifice for our household and even some nail-biting times with our backs to the wall. Inevitably, we even needed to refinance our house in order to stay housed and not lose our home. Unfortunately, we had not been able to establish a "safety net" because all our extra funds were going to the 55th Street Project. Honestly, it was definitely something I didn't imagine us going through as first time home-buyers.

Every penny had to be stretched until it hurt. And it did! By then we were pregnant with our second child. Chicken and Beef Top Ramen as well as various pasta dishes became a staple in our home versus steak and potatoes. Thankfully, I had a loving mother who graciously supplied my family with food or delicious home-cooked meals a few days a week. She never had any idea what a blessing her meals were, since I didn't share with her the extreme financial burden we were under. Quite frankly she was in the midst of fighting breast cancer and I didn't want her to have any other worries on her mind regarding my situation. She needed to focus on herself.

Also, there is no greater sacrifice a black woman can make than when it comes to the care of her hair. I paid the ultimate sacrifice! My hair appointments dwindled down from bi-weekly to every 6-8 weeks. My hairstyles went from glamorous to a simple, single pulled-back ponytail. There were also no more salon mani-pedis. I found myself doing my own feet and nails as I was able, being a working mother of two small children. In the end, all the sacrifices we made were worth it. Years have gone by but the building we all poured our blood, sweat, and tears into still stands and I have such a feeling of accomplishment driving by with my children, pointing to our building and saying, "Yeah, we built that!"

Jamal - The Marching Order King

I remember calling Lynee one night about the refinancing of our 55th Street project. I had come to the realization that if Lynee and I did not go all out and put in over 100 percent effort, this project was DOA, (Dead on Arrival). Keith and I would work all day at our day jobs, go to the project around 5:30 pm and work up to 10:00 pm three to four days a week. We would pay the 55th Street mortgage before paying our own mortgage. That's what I call commitment! I remember feeling so exposed to the fact that we could lose this property and the pain it would cause if we didn't see this thing through.

I also remember that we had our second Unique BBQ at the Egypt Theater in Oakland. This time around we decided to only make it a one-day event on Saturday so none of us would have to miss work on Friday. It was another beautiful hot summer day in Oakland as we set up shop for the day. The menu consisted of BBQ chicken, ribs, potato salad, green beans and a slice or two of wheat bread. The smell of master chef Keith's BBQ wafted through the summer air. We could not have picked a better day for a BBQ, I thought. However, as our fundraiser got underway there was drama in the neighborhood that could have impeded our efforts of having a successful outcome. For starters there was a fight where someone got "laid out" in the street. A fire hydrant was opened causing all traffic to be halted due to the water that flooded the street. The police were called multiple times for a group of young people that jumped on top of one of the city's AC Transit buses that was making its way down the street. Through it all, all the partners kept their focus on the fundraising goal. The moral of the story is: "Keep your eyes on the prize."

Mary - The Visionary

I recall clearly thinking that my time and finances no longer belonged to me. After doing a full day at the office where I had many responsibilities and a large group of people to mentor, oversee and nurture, the rest of my waking hours had to be spent either at the property putting on door stops, working joint compound, or doing whatever there was to do to help this project move along and get finished. I remember some of our meetings were tense and even heartbreaking when we discovered that someone had quit the project. However, the partner that quit only quit for a day or two and then got right back "on the horse" with renewed strength leaving room for the next partner to quit for a few days. What a time we had together!

We most certainly do not want anyone to think that it was all bad. We had great fun. One remembrance was a great breakfast at a recreation center where we came together just to have good food and fellowship with our families and friends. We are so very blessed to have a chef in our midst that can prepare any meal fit for any King and/or Queen! On our 10th anniversary together, after the building was sold and things had sort of settled back to normal, we got all gussied up in our Sunday best, hired a limo and went to have dinner at one of the best restaurants in San Francisco, CA. That was a special evening!

Each of the partners learned and added something to their portfolio. One partner takes great pride in being able to say that "if you need to put in door stops", let us know. Another partner became effective in hanging and re-hanging kitchen cabinets. As we were doing chores, we sometimes had to re-do, install and uninstall and install again before it was done correctly. Again, as one of my mentors often said "if you haven't been to Chicago you just haven't been". Believe me, none of us had ever been involved in this type of project before, but oh, how we learned and learned quickly!

Meredith – The Project Manager

My journey began in finance long before the thought of joining this group. As I recall, I received an invitation to attend a business opportunity meeting/presentation and to partake in a discussion about an opportunity to join with other like-minded individuals. The Group was known as Plan 1994 later to be re-named Unique Enterprises. This concept to join an Investment Club was very interesting to me. The room was filled with familiar and some unfamiliar faces, nevertheless the energy in the room felt positive. As the concept was presented, I thought to myself could this be a way to create financial stability? My last thought was "Together we stand, divided we fall" so I said yes I'll give it a try. After 25 years, I'm still a member.

Robin - The Tie That Binds

I remember the many challenges, roadblocks, lost memberships and "rainy days" we faced during the time when we were diligently trying to get through that "ever-so-long" project. The struggle that each of us (per person and per household) had to endure each month coming up with our dues was more than the average person could take. As I remember, we had just bought our home and were getting used to paying our mortgage and were terrified not to "mess this up" since it was our first big purchase. Our children were growing like weeds and as they grew, so did their needs inclusive of school tuition, school clothes, uniforms, school supplies and so many other requests and requirements as well as trying to maintain some sort of lifestyle that would allow for vacations and family time with them which we committed to doing on a yearly basis.

Oh, the many thoughts in my head telling me there were a plethora of other things you should be thinking about and wanted to do but squeezed through the thought and energy to push on to complete the project anyway. God only knows how we were able to continue loving and respecting each other (as much as we could, though the struggle was real). We have had our tolerance tried and our degree of restraints tested with those we had to deal with trying to finish this endeavor but I have seen firsthand that with God, ALL things are possible even when the odds are stacked against you.

All throughout that rollercoaster ride of highs and lows, we ended with the great feeling of knowing that you can stand the test of time so that you can get to "The Blessing". Not only did we weather tough times together, we did on our own individual lives, and we were all able to purchase homes as well. We had to trust God to take care of our families while we weathered this and we held each other up, we pushed through, and we prayed, A LOT, because we knew we had no other choice. We were not going down without a fight! God is AMAZING and seeing His favor manifested in our lives was so rewarding. Many would ask "how did we do it?" The answer is PERSEVERANCE!!!! It is certainly true of the statement, "no test, no testimony"!

Not only were there remembrances of hard knocks but pleasant and happy times during all of this as we laughed to keep from crying because we were sure no one would believe all the hurdles we jumped or hoops we had to leap through. We would get through one thing and sure enough there was something coming right behind it. But then it would be followed by yet another victory and we would reward ourselves by celebrating with dinner at nice eating establishments laughing hysterically at what we just went through!

We were so grateful for those times and I might add, proud of ourselves as well for sticking with the course!!! The supporters we had from our lenders to our friends and family were rooting for us and waiting in anticipation of our completed mission and to know that, was an amazing feeling!

William - The Wild Card

In just about every card game we know and other games, there is always a piece or card that would enable you to "win a hand" or the game. These are called "Wild Card" pieces or cards that gives one the ability to use them to get ahead or even win when it appears that all may be lost. I remember my employer who was in the non-profit development business, talking about this vacant lot and saying that they were not going to pursue it. As a partner of an investment group who had a little nest egg, I thought it was a great opportunity. I called the owner of the lot and negotiated a price of $35,000. I talked with a friend who was in the real estate finance business and he informed me that we could get financed not only to purchase the lot, but to put up the building as well. After talking with the partners, it was decided that the price was not a bad deal to get our real estate baby going. My source let us know that since the organization was not credit-worthy, we would have to utilize the credit of one or all of our members. After discussion and credit submission among the partners, one partner was able to qualify and we were given a loan to purchase and build our development dream.

Just as the biblical children of Israel took a 40 year journey in the wilderness that should have taken 4 days, we took a 4 year journey to build a building that should have taken 4 months. Along the way we hired, trained and got to know house inspectors, real estate appraisers, multiple contractors and subcontractors, mortgage bankers, police detectives and learned patience and persistence within and among the membership. During this time that "tries men's souls" and builds character, I was threatened with expulsion and even death many times (LOL). I always kept in my mind that we are an investment group that wants to build wealth within our membership, our families and our communities. As soon as the building was completed the first words out of my mouth were "SELL THE BUILDING!" to which I was promptly discouraged, censored, vetoed and plain old ignored. However, after four years of being a landlord and the challenges that it did bring, we sold the building for a handsome return on our investment. Without this "Wild Card" mentality Unique Enterprises of Oakland would not have enjoyed a large return on our real estate investment!

Lynée - The Family

I remember the seemingly endless trips to Home Depot. Eventually all of the members were asked to apply for a credit card so that anybody could go and pick up items when needed. Of course, when we needed them, you were usually short on cash so you HAD to use a credit card. The APR (annual percentage rate) was outrageous, of course, but after a while, you just ignored it so we could get the building completed.

Our members went to Home Depot so often, we got to know the staff really well. During that time, I learned more than I ever thought I would about the joint compound that was so heavy, I had to drive slowly because my car was small and it would make the car lower to the ground! In one particular instance, I remember going to the store to buy and pick up internal doors with Madeline. We didn't have a truck, so we put them on top of the roof of the car and rode back slowly to the property, each of us with our hands out of the window to hold the doors in place so they didn't fall off the car. We kept saying one day we're going to laugh about this but right now, this is crazy! Thank God we still laugh about it.

The disappointment and disgust of reading proposals from contractor after contractor, listening to and being failed by them time and time again. They would usually downplay the work of the previous contractor, say he could fix it or do it better, then mess up his job as well. After a while, Unique got really good at firing contractors. I suppose you could say we became our own general contractors. We end up finishing the project ourselves and coming out with an amazing building! To this day, the thought of working with a contractor makes me shudder a little, after I finish rolling my eyes…but I must say I can't wait for the day that I meet one that will do what they say, on time, on budget and with quality workmanship.

Keith - The Quiet Storm

As with any life experience, I look back on it with a myriad of emotions that have shaped my thinking in how I see things. Also, I recall plenty of invaluable lessons that were taught through this experience. Through the years of involvement in this group, so many memorable things come to mind. There were many wonderful positive recollections, but also a few bitter memories as well. Therefore, I won't go into too much detail about the specifics of what I remember but the emotion behind the event.

Hopeful *("Oh please God...")* - When I was approached about this idea and then later deciding to get involved, I was naively hopeful that this would work. There is a saying in the MLM (Multi-Level Marketing) world that I always unknowingly bought into. It's a simple idea that states; "It's better to have 1% of 100 people's efforts than 100% of my own effort." I believed then as I do now, that there is nothing that a motivated, dedicated, faithful and faith-filled (yes, there is a difference!) group of people can't accomplish.

Excitement *("3, 2, 1, BLASTOFF!!!...")* - The very 1st meeting of this idea of a group of people to come together for the purpose of building wealth was an exciting concept to me. I remember that first concept meeting of over 25 people and thinking how exciting our journey together is going to be. Other exciting times come to mind when I think about how we secured the loan for our construction project (see "Surprise"), and then actually breaking ground.

Frustration *("Oh, COME ON!!!...")* - Whenever you are trying to do something to get ahead and you are dependent on others to do their part, frustration is always going to be a spoke in the wheel. So many elements added to the frustration we all felt: the city that didn't want to approve our plans, the contractors that did not keep their promises, we even experienced frustration amongst each other. With all that being said, frustration can and does cause many to "throw in the towel." Even in writing this book, we have had a level of challenges that frustrate. As you might surmise, none of us have ever attempted to write a book before. Just like our land project, what was supposed to take 6 months took 4+ years. The few pages of this book you would think from its length could be written in a few days or weeks but has actually taken years and is the culmination of not just experiences but real feelings.

Surprise *("WTH?!?...")* - As prepared as we thought we were for the trek ahead of us, when you go on a journey for the first time you will undoubtedly encounter some surprises along the way. A memorable surprise occurred in our stock trading that helped us on our way to acquiring our first property. As a group we were novices (to put it generously) in trading stock. A few of us may have had a little experience, but really just enough experience to get into trouble. We made our investment choices from companies we thought were doing well and companies that were popular at the time. In evaluating a company as a potential investment, none of us really understood the procedure and significance of reading and comprehending earnings reports, profit & earnings ratios, revenues, balance sheets, profit & loss statements, and so on. While we knew that this information is important in making good choices, it was all just numbers on a page to us. Thank God we were investing in a time where you really didn't need to be a Wall Street guru to have success. It wasn't important that we fully understood the game, it was only important that we were in the game. The momentum behind online companies was just starting to take off. It seemed like any company that put ".com" at the end of its name took off like a rocket. Prior to the dot com bubble bursting, these stocks would commonly appreciate 5, 10, 20, even 100 fold seemingly overnight. One such stock was a company called ONSALE.com. I remember choosing it because it was a website I would commonly use to purchase computer hardware for my business. They seemed to be doing a good business and at the time their stock was trading under $5 per share. Given our limited resources at the time, the under $5 per share part looked really good as we could get a good number of shares with the amount of funds we were working with. I remember getting the call from one of the other partners. In a very excited tone I heard them say…

"MAN, KEITH! DID YOU CHECK THE STOCKS TODAY?!?... YOU SEE WHAT'S GOING ON WITH ONSALE? ...IT'S UP OVER $107 PER SHARE!!!"

To say the least we were all pleasantly caught off guard with this. Because we didn't daily check the activity of the stocks we picked, in looking at the history, we were very surprised to see that in the matter of a few trading days ONSALE.com ballooned from $5 - $7 per share to $105 - $113 per share. We paid very close attention to it at that point and when it started to decline back, we sold it for a very nice profit. ONSALE.com like many of the other popup dot com websites never got back to those inflated highs. Many .coms like Amazon, Netflix and EBAY are still viable to this day. I recently found out that Amazon.com started in 1994… the same year Unique Enterprises organized. Talk about "Oh what if…"

Another pleasant surprise was the loan approval for the capital to purchase our plot of land and ultimately build thereupon. While the funds from the ONSALE.com transaction got us to the ballgame, we still needed more funds to actually play. It was mentioned earlier how we all had our credit run to see if anyone qualified for a loan. Lo and behold I was approved for $135,000 that we thought would be enough to complete our project. However, due to many mishaps and missteps, we would need more capital.

Our first two tenants were a delight and one was able to move out when she was able to buy a house of her own. The renter we allowed to move in from her departure provided us with a couple of unpleasant surprises. To be fair, this first incident was not the fault of our new tenant but it occurred at their unit so maybe it was a foreshadowing of things to come. So, one day we received a call from our new occupant that the front door needed to be replaced. WHAT!?! It turned out that the police were involved in chasing someone they believed to be a drug dealer. The suspect ran down the side of our property and jumped a fence to try to escape. The authorities in their pursuit and search had kicked the front door in because they believed the suspect was hiding inside. The door and the frame sustained significant damage. The door and locks needed to be replaced and the door frame repaired. The next surprise came about as we were in the middle of the transaction to sell the building. As the prospective buyer was conducting his inspection, mold was discovered in the wall shared by the garage. It turned out the tenant had brought her washing machine from her previous residence to our place but she neglected to connect the hose to drain the water out. The moisture from the machine caused mold on the adjacent wall and some on the wall to the connecting apartment that had to be repaired before the sale could go through. In repairing the moldy wall we discovered baby mice in the wall. Our exterminator informed us that the reason we had mice was due to the "backyard buffet" caused by an apple tree and the fallen fruit.

Gratitude *('Thank you LORD!...")* - Thankful is the only thing I can be as I think back on all our ups, downs, frustrations and blessings. The fact that we have not killed each other or have a spirit of ill will toward one another is a blessing that I don't take for granted. When you go into business with friends and money is being exchanged (large or small), it's very easy for misunderstandings, hurt feelings, and strong opinions to dominate and bring about divisions. While there were some tense moments at times and everything was not 100% buy in, I never felt like we disrespected each other's position or ideas. I am grateful to God that through it all we were able to maintain our love for each other and not allow our quest for investment success to turn us into people that can't get along or stand to be in each other's company. Another observation that I am grateful about is the fact that in the middle of the time when we were paying almost $300 additional dollars per member on a mortgage for a building that was not even halfway finished, ALL of us were able to become homeowners. To this day, I marvel at what God was doing because it didn't make any sense for all us to be able to do that. GOD IS AMAZING!

Shock *("How did that happen?!?...")* -Looking back on our 2nd and 3rd loan approvals was a moment of shock in retrospect. At the time we just thought it was a normal part of the process but as we found out later, this was another instance and opportunity to appreciate how God works things out. Sometimes not knowing what you need to know allows you to "just do it" and walk by faith. When we got our 1st loan to purchase the lot and start construction, unbeknown to us, our lender knew ahead of time that we would need more capital and when we went to them for additional funds the paperwork was already in place and only had to be signed. The 3rd loan was the amazing one. Due to contractor foul ups and mismanagement, even the additional funds from the 2nd loan was not enough and our 1st lender was not willing to extend us any more capital. We needed another lender and God sent a gentleman (a mortgage broker) to cross paths with Jamal and we secured our next lender. We were approved for our 3rd loan and had the capital to finally complete our project. The shock came after the loan was approved and the funds in hand. Our 2nd lender said, in all his years of doing loans, he has never seen a conventional loan approved when the structure is not completed yet. So in essence we were able to refinance a higher interest construction loan into a lower interest conventional loan while the collateral in question is still under construction! We didn't know that but apparently this was not a normal practice. From our standpoint, nothing about this endeavor was "normal." All our 2nd lender could say to Jamal after the loan had gone through was "I don't know what God you guys are praying to, but you guys need to keep praying to and praising him!" - AMEN, Brother!

Intolerance *("Just GET IT DONE!!!...")* - I remember vividly the frustration that came with watching our incomplete structure sitting in the elements day after day, week after week, month after month. After this experience, contractors have left a bad taste in our mouths for any future jobs we may use them for. For this project they seemed to make big promises on what they could do but then fell short on the delivery. Also, each one would criticize the work of the previous contractor, which we all found annoying and disrespectful. They would have excuse after excuse on why something was not finished and would always need more money. In the final stages Jamal and I would go in after work and finish the work ourselves working late into the evenings. You know the old adage on wanting something done right...

Pride *(Yeah, WE BAD!...)* - The sense of pride and accomplishment was immeasurable when the building was complete. Here we were, a group of inexperienced people that came together to do something none of us had ever done before. We were not just investing and raising funds, we were collectively applying for loans, negotiating contracts, hiring contractors, firing contractors and even getting hands on experience through the sweat equity we all put into keeping the ball rolling. Other "professionals" in the real estate game gave us little chance of being successful in what we were trying to do but for us to see this project to its completion gave us all a measure of high esteem.

Shame *(yeah, we're bad!...)* - I'd be only telling one side if I didn't mention some of our unsound (read: DUMB!) investments. As I look back over a few, I can only ask myself "what were we thinking?!?" I think it was part of our learning process on what NOT to do. We learned a few expensive lessons but in the end I believe it made us shrewder investors. One such poor "investment" was a pyramid (ponzi) scheme called "Friends Helping Friends". To our defense this was the 1st time any of us heard of anything like this and we had the testimony of a few that had some measure of success in it. If I recall correctly we invested $1,200 to "help a friend" and when it was our turn to be "helped" we would in turn receive $1,200 from 8 other "investors" for a net of something like $9,500 after club fees were paid. Our naivete cost us $1,200 but the lesson learned going forward was well received. Another lesson I'm sorry(and embarrassed) to say cost us in the low 5 figures. After cashing out on our building project we had substantial capital for our next endeavor. We all agreed that we should not put all our eggs in one basket and we should diversify among a number of investments. One such investment came about when we were approached by someone (a contractor of all people) a member of our group had worked with in the past on other projects. The details are kind of sketchy, being so long ago, but he needed some funds to either complete construction or to cover closing costs on a loan. Since we were in that same situation with our project, we had empathy for the situation. Long story short, we were never repaid for our investment and the structure of our loan paperwork with the other party was not really strong enough for us to enforce any significant action. Another expensive lesson learned! There were a few others but I think you get the idea of some of the mistakes we made. For me I look at this as us paying our tuition to the college of "Life In Business".

Unity *(WE ALL WE GOT!...)* - As stated earlier in the Gratitude section, I praise God for the oneness this group has displayed over the years. Not all of our decisions were unanimous. Sometimes we had to come to the conclusion to agree to disagree. When it came time for action, we were always on one accord pulling in the same direction. An example would be in our fundraising efforts. We did yard sales, concerts, sold barbecue dinners, among other things. Sometimes members would have to take time off from work or make other commitments of time, energy or even money to realize the objective at hand. I truly believe that the unity of TEAM (Together Everyone Achieves More) and our faith in God enabled us to go through and grow through many of the obstacles we faced and honestly are still facing.

    Euphoria *("$...CHA - CHING!!!...$...")* - You can only imagine the feeling of excitement, joy, elation, jubilation, and delight among other adjectives when we first, completed the building, second, when we started receiving rents, and third when we sold the building. Upon completion we immediately realized that instead of continually shelling out money to pay for this building, the building could now pay us for a while. We also realized that we had a capital fixed asset on our books. When we sold the building, it was a bittersweet moment for me. While many in the group were excited about the prospect of closing the chapter on this project and moving on to something else, personally, I would have loved to keep the property and keep receiving a monthly income. In any case, to cash out of our project after the years of drama behind it was an incredible time. We started with

$10,000 from our own pockets and fundraisers and grew it to mid 6 figures by the grace of God!.

"Every great dream begins with a dreamer: always remember you have within you the strength, the patience, and the passion to reach for the stars to change the world"

Harriet Tubman

Chapter 9

Blessings

In the middle of this project we realized that we experienced many, many blessings; therefore, we want to share some of them. When most people think of blessings, the first thing that comes to mind is something that made the heart feel exceedingly glad. There were times we had to look much deeper and longer to see the real blessings in this project. Even in our struggles, we came to understand and find blessings in situations no matter how upside down or wrong the situation looked at the time.

So where are the blessings? One blessing that has come from the Unique story is one of being able to convey a story of trial and triumph. A story where African American people came together physically, financially, emotionally, mentally, spiritually and were blessed to build, rent, sell and split the proceeds of a real estate investment. To have a story of success, in a time where success is not necessarily the norm in the real estate marketplace, we feel it is a blessing. This story can assist you in knowing that "if you can do it once, you can do it again." Like the gospel song says…"each victory will help you some other to win!"[5]

Believe it or not, one of our major blessings was trusting a person's INCORRECT INFORMATION. How was that a blessing? Well, we believed we had examined the report presented to us when we were approached by an unforeseen situation that cautioned us to look a little closer. AFTER we had a complaint about the property line, we learned that we actually had more property than we had originally thought and the individual who complained had less property!!! What an unexpected blessing!! When you recognize your errors, investigate more and seek professional advice, you may be pleased to find that it is well worth checking further even if the recommendation did not come from a trusted source.

Of course we had some "exceedingly glad" blessings. We were blessed with new marriages while the more seasoned marriages became stronger. New babies were born and our partners were even able to purchase personal property. We felt the favor of God all around us both collectively and personally.

We were also blessed to meet many, many, many new and interesting people, some of which became lifelong friends and associates. On our journey, we met an amazing financial expert who was experienced in making and packaging the kind of loan we needed but probably did not know we needed at the time. He was a man in whom we can trust. Even in the way he came into our lives was a blessing. One of our partners was listening to a new business network radio station and heard about him and decided to give him a call. What a blessing he was to us professionally and personally as we were able to utilize his knowledge and expertise in loan options to our benefit. Once the building sold, we re-paid our debt list and dividends were distributed.

"If thou faint in the day of adversity,
thy strength is small"
Proverbs 24:10

Chapter 10
<u>Our Journey Continues</u>

It is our sincere hope that you have enjoyed reading our book. We are hoping that our story has given you the inspiration perhaps to form your own investment group while avoiding the pitfalls and challenges we faced. It is our desire that you will encourage others to read this book as well. Some of you may be wondering about us and asking yourselves what's currently going on with Unique. Happy are we to give you a sneak peek at us today. As of this writing, we must say right away, we have not developed another property from the ground up; however, we have made other property investments that were nowhere near as stressful. Many things have happened since 1994 when we began this journey that we told you about in this book. The technological capabilities today are more than we could have imagined. Communication seems to be at the "speed of light" or faster these days. We are now able to have meetings via telecommunication which we take every opportunity to do, especially since our members live in different geographical locations. Our meeting minutes are no longer printed on paper but can now be recorded and viewed at the partner's leisure time and discretion. However, we still enjoy our in person meetings together and that seems to work best for this group. Let's face it; it would be difficult for us to have our snacks and meals together if we were not in the same space. This group truly enjoys eating! Today, Unique members can be found a little more spread out as three of our members have ventured into other parts of California, but we get together whenever we can and still have our weekly Zoom conference calls to stay connected and conduct business.

Unique is now twenty-five plus years old and all grown up. As we've told you earlier, we have had weddings and births together. Various illnesses, cancer, stroke, heart failure, diabetes, a traumatic car accident of one of our partners and more have invaded this group and we even endured loved ones' transitions from this life to a new and eternal one. Through it all we have remained together and, by God's grace, no divorces. What a blessing!

It's unbelievable that we had very young children when our journey began but now we would like to tell you what some of the "children" of this group are currently doing.

Our Music Man

William "Aaron" Randolph V began his career as a drummer at the tender age of two years old playing on pots and pans. To no one's surprise, he soon became the drummer for his school's band and also his church choir before later forming his own band, The St. Valentinez for which William was lead vocalist and director. The group performed at many Bay Area venues and have had a large following. The St. Valentinez released their first LP in 2014. William attended the prestigious Berklee School of Music in Boston, Massachusetts where he continued to work on his gift. Today, at 29 years of age, he is busy working on his new found passion in music production. William was a part of the musical team for a hip hop musical comedy entitled "Co-Founders" that was presented at Joe's Pub in New York in the Spring of 2022. William has collaborated on many projects with local artists and recently released a music video with Oakland's Jada Imani entitled "Rosa Parks. He has received recognition for the music production for KQED's "If Cities Could Dance, Oakland Boogaloo", for which his father, William, aka "The Wild Card", starred in. He continues to add to his growing list of accomplishments. We are sure you will hear about him in the near future.

Our Cameraman

Joshua McClinton fell in love with motion pictures at the age of 6 after seeing his first "Spiderman" movie on the big screen. Shortly after this exposure, he had an interest in seeing every superhero movie that was released. Joshua's creativity prospered once we purchased a small handheld "Flip" video camera for him. He loved videotaping himself and his friends doing crazy stunts around the house or in the backyard. In 2009, his movie making became an avenue of healing that helped him to get through his grief after losing his grandmother and aunt to breast cancer. He worked with a volunteer UCLA film graduate to create a video about the grief support program he and other kids were participants of. The video turned out to be a very moving experience and highlighted the program in a positive light. In his pre-teens, his interest in film escalated as he discovered websites on the internet about making movies or trailers of upcoming movies. Joshua graduated in June 2016 from the SLAM (San Leandro Academy for Multimedia). He won two Slammy Awards for Best Narrative and Best Slideshow in 2015-2016 as well as a SLED (San Leandro Education) Shortie for Best Short Film (2016).

He began taking classes in Media Arts at a city college, but soon realized he needed to take another path to his dreams. He left home before his 18th birthday to set out on his quest as an artist in Los Angeles, California. He has worked as a photographer and videographer with rappers and designers and has traveled on tours in the U.S. as well as Paris and Japan. Today Joshua is behind the camera constantly honing his skills and discovering more layers about himself in video production, editing, photography, music and media arts. The 2020 Pandemic became a year of deep reflection and self-discovery for Josh regarding his Christian faith. He started and leads an online Bible study ministry to reach out to his peers and is partnering with other men and women of faith to start a company called VOY (Voices of Yahweh) to use his media arts skills to passionately reach the youth of this generation with the Gospel of Jesus Christ through film and music.

Our Athlete – Excelling in Sports/Future Nurse

Elianna McClinton was destined to play sports from the day she was born. Upon examination, her doctor remarked that she had an athletic body and was bowlegged. Hence, any ball that Eli got into her hands she excelled in. Her first sport was soccer at the age of 6 and she took off like a jet to make her first goal and more subsequently. We thought we had a little soccer star in the making, but the following year she changed course and joined a girls' softball league. In her first year playing softball, her team the Red Hot Chili Peppers took the championship for their division. Her coach gave her the nickname "Speedy Pepper". Needless to say, Elianna was smitten with the game of softball and played for 8 more years in recreational and competitive leagues up until high school in the positions of pitcher, shortstop, and second baseman. She also decided to give basketball a try in middle school and earned a position as a point guard on the varsity girl's team for 3 years. After middle school, she played on both the varsity girl's basketball and softball teams for her high school. She proudly received 2 varsity letters as a scholar-athlete at the end of her freshman year in high school. However, Elianna hung up her cleats after graduating high school in 2018 and is currently a senior pursuing a BSN (Bachelor of Science in Nursing) degree at a college in the Midwest.

Her goal is to work in underprivileged communities with patients in hospitals as a traveling Emergency Room nurse. She was hired as a CNA (Certified Nursing Assistant) for a local hospital in 2021 and is looking forward to the opportunity to learn and build on her nursing skills as she works with various patients and continues in her studies. In addition, Elianna (aka "El") loves working with her brother Joshua (Imjahshua) singing and performing Christian rap songs composed by him and his partner Scotty Summer. In 2020, they made a music video together. To her utter surprise their first song together "Thunder Cry"; was uploaded to her brother's YouTube Channel, Sicology, and received over 50K views. Eli also has a heart for reaching her generation with the Gospel of Jesus Christ as a member of CRU (Campus Crusade for Christ) and participated in mission trips in Mexico, in the past and most recently in Costa Rico and the heart of a Detroit neighborhood to share the Good News with children and adults.

Our Cosmetologist, Fashion Blogger

Leslie "Nikki" Randolph - After graduating from high school, Leslie attended and completed her studies in cosmetology from Alameda Beauty College and shortly after, she passed the exam to receive her license from the California Board of Cosmetology. After receiving her license, she began working for Viveur Salon in Berkeley, California. Leslie later decided to enroll in Carrington College where she completed her courses and received her certificate in Medical Billing and Coding. Soon after graduation, Leslie began working full-time at Associated Orthopedic Surgeons in Castro Valley, California where she worked several years before obtaining employment at John Muir Medical Center in San Ramon, California. Although Leslie has worked mostly in the corporate world, she has always had a passion for fashion and has become a fashion blogger and personal stylist to local artists and models and is working towards having a full-time life doing what she loves. She is a proud mother to a 14-year-old 4.0 high school student who inspires to one day walk the halls of Howard University.

Our Educator

Mia Randolph - Miz Mia, as she is affectionately called, graduated from Sacramento State University with a BA degree in Child Development. Her decision to work with children was not a surprise to her parents as she has always been drawn to "the babies". While in college, Mia began her career nurturing and educating the infant/toddler, preschool and school age children until she ventured on to open and operate "Miz Mia's Kidz", her very own licensed in-home child care where she cared for numerous children of various ages. Unique was especially proud and more than happy to sow a seed into one of our own. At the height of the economic crisis, Miz Mia closed her doors and went back to the classroom, working with school age children in a before and after school program for San Juan Unified School District. Later, Mia took on a new challenge when she obtained a TOSA (Teacher On Special Assignment) position where she would mentor, coach and facilitate professional learning opportunities and strategies for teachers and support staff in the areas of behavior management, classroom environment, curriculum, assessments and other topics that promote the achievement of staff, children and their families. After completing her assignment as TOSA, Mia returned to the classroom once again for a brief time before obtaining an administrative position while studying to receive her credentials that will allow her to assist in the needs of the children and teachers beyond the classroom.

Our Dental Assistant

Jasmine, started and completed the dental assistant program at Carrington College. She has worked at one of the renowned dental offices in San Francisco, CA. She is a registered dental assistant ready to take the test to specialize in pediatric dental care as she has a strong love for children and a natural aptitude to work with them. She has had many accolades from parents in how she handles the children and the calming effect she has on her young patients. She has even had some write ups in social media.

Our Cosmetologist

Jessica Marie is a graduate from Georgia Southern University located in Statesboro, Ga. In 2017 she earned her Bachelors of Arts degree in Psychology. Shortly after graduating she began working at The Children's Clinic of Atlanta where she worked as a Case Manager.

Upon relocating back to California in 2019, Jessica decided to continue her studies in cosmetology with the intention to pursue her dream of becoming a licensed cosmetologist. In 2020, Jessica was able to pass the exam and received her cosmetology license, which was issued by the California Board of Cosmetology. This comes as no surprise as she has always been interested in hair care. As a toddler I can remember her saying "Mom I'm gonna do me some hair". Her love for hair care has led her to continue the journey and is now the proud owner and operator of her very 1st Salon Suite specializing in natural hair care and wig design. The branded name for her salon is "Hair by J Marie".

As a small business owner of Hair by J. Marie, her goal is to own several salon suites that offer a variety of hair care services.

Who Are We?

Unique Enterprises Partners

We want to take this time to introduce you to the "*Unique*" members…

Mary – The Visionary

My covenant with Unique began long before January 1994, long before I knew the name. I wish I could pinpoint the day and time I began this awesome journey with this group, but for the life of me, I can't.

I wish I could tell you that it began while working in Corporate America, on one payday that happened to be a Friday. While most of my co-workers were out at restaurants or in one of the wonderful stores in Union Square shopping, I decided to stay in the office when I happened to walk in the lunchroom and noticed a relatively small group of my Asian co-workers at their usual table eating the lunches they brought from home. However, this time something was different that I had never noticed before. On this particular day, they were quietly exchanging money. I walked over to the table and asked "what are y'all doing?" They graciously gave me the short version of what was happening. Of course, I continued to press until I got a better version. By the way, I could do that because at that time I was the Manager of some of them. Yet, I still don't know if that stirred me in any way but it definitely made me think about it more and more.

I wish I could tell you that this journey began when I heard and read about and looked into the story of King David and his son Solomon. King David set in motion plans for the building of the Temple; he drew up the blueprints, surveyed the land, and collected the construction materials. His son Solomon then picked up all the plans his father had set in motion and continued to get the Temple built. Yet, I still don't know if that was the deciding moment for me but God was still working His plan within me.

I believe that I always knew that I had to leave something behind, something I later learned was called a *legacy*, for the two fruits of my womb, my daughter and son, I wanted to leave something that they could build on. Of course, I had no clue how to do this and I didn't know if "legacies" could be bought by the pound, bushel, inches or yard, but I knew I had to have it and leave one.

One day I looked around and realized I was impregnated with a vision that I knew that somehow and someday I had to give birth to it. After a while or better yet, after I had the nerve, I began to vocalize my thoughts to whomever I had the opportunity to speak to. Sometimes it made sense and sometimes not, then finally I got through to a few people the vision I thought I had in mind. What have I learned from this extraordinary journey? I'm so glad you asked. I have learned many, many things but since I do not want to bore you with so many, I will tell you two great things. First, I have learned to trust others with my resources, time and energy. Second, I have learned to let love be without dissimulation (let love abide). Let me tell you those things were not and are not easy to learn for many reasons.

Who would have ever thought that a scared, shy, bashful, unassuming, undereducated young woman from the backwoods of Sunflower County, Mississippi would become a matriarch, a visionary, a teacher, a dreamer, a leader, an instrument of God's vision for my legacy and a queen? Who knew? The God I have chosen to honor and serve knew, as He is unique and whatever His soul desires, that He does, and He has and is performing in my life what He has appointed for me. However, my most cherished position in this group is resting in the sweet knowledge that "I am just one of eight!"

Meredith - The Project Manager

I am Meredith Evans-Moore, a wife, mother and "one of eight" of Unique Enterprises.

Recently I retired from Oakland Unified School District and the City of Oakland Parks and Recreation Department. My Career as an instructor began well over 40 years ago as a substitute Instructional Assistant better known as A ParaProfessional. After spending several years working in the Early Childhood Program, I was encouraged to continue my education and pursue an ECE (Early Childhood Education) permit to instruct children. I'm proud to say I obtained several levels of permits from Assistant Aid to Site Supervisor. During that time, I attended Cal State University of Hayward (now named Cal State East Bay), Merritt College and Chabot College. I also studied Business Administration, Finance, and Project Management. My love for organizing programs and managing projects led me to create Magic 6 Travel Company, join various groups, and I recently began studying stock market investments. I am passionate about yielding results in every program, investment, leadership role and educational endeavor. Above all, I enjoy working with people and have dedicated most of my career to the education and development of young people and their families.

I am proud to be an active member of Unique Enterprises, an investment club of like- minded individuals that strive to educate, invest and create financial gain. One of our goals is to leave a legacy for those who will follow in our footsteps.

Keith - The Quiet Storm

I was a 30 year old I.T. professional working for a computer manufacturer in the Silicon Valley, when Unique Enterprises began in 1994 . Mary(Our Visionary) came to my wife, Lynée and I with the idea to get a group of people together for the purpose of pooling money for investment purposes and I was all in, because I knew that many wealthy people acquired their wealth through sound investing. I felt the possibilities were unlimited for a group of like-minded people to pool their funds together for the purpose of creating wealth. The only thing holding back people like myself and others was 1) capital and 2) knowledge or the lack thereof. I also knew that it wouldn't take a whole lot to get started and a group of people putting their pennies together would take care of the capital. That left knowledge that I did not have. I envisioned our meetings being learning sessions where collectively we would be "in school" so to speak; learning and gaining the education we needed to have to take us to the next level.

I also knew that when it came to dealing with people that look like me and when money is involved, it can and often does get messy. So while I was onboard, I didn't want to be negative on the prospect, I know my people can be petty and messy when a few dollars are involved. Questions might arise like, "who's gonna hold the money?" or "why should we invest in this or that?" In my mind the task at hand was; how could a group of individuals with different philosophies, backgrounds, educational levels, and monetary abilities come together and be in agreement on the multitude of investment avenues that would be at our disposal?

As I recall, at the first get acquainted meeting, there were 23 people in attendance, many of whom I was close to but others not so much. Money can ruin relationships and I didn't want arguments over investment ideas or money to sour relationships. As it turned out, there have been funny times and sad times. There have been times when our patience, friendship and faith have been stretched and tested to the breaking point. I truly believe that the bonds that have been created through all of our ups and downs are bonds that will never be broken. Would I change any of what we went through? Maybe. One thing I have learned through it all is that when the chips are down and I am between a rock and a hard place, there are seven other people that will go through the fire with me and that is very reassuring.

Lynée - The Family

My name is Lynée and I joined *Unique*, because my mother is the visionary and founder and I wanted to show her my support as well as building a strong financial legacy. At that time I was working at the Pacific Bell Yellow Pages and my husband and I had recently bought our first home. I was excited to join my mother's venture and help bring her idea to fruition. I had no idea what I would learn and how the Unique members would become such a cornerstone in my life.

I believe that when the right people come together you can accomplish great things. I continue to stay with Unique because we are family. It has always been family and with each growing year we become even closer. Through this process, babies and grandbabies were born, anniversaries celebrated and untold shared time together where we laughed, cried and learned together.

Despite how ridiculously hard it had gotten, I just refused to quit and it helped in many areas in my life. I learned not to give up. I have found when you stick together that you can get anything done and that's what is keeping me with Unique. The things that I have learned have manifested itself in many areas of my life. In order to go to the next level, I had to grow through the experiences in order to achieve my next level with *Unique Enterprises*.

<u>William - The Wild Card</u>

My name is William R. Randolph III, my "Unique Experience" began one afternoon when I received a telephone call from Mary F. Tuft. Mary called me to inform me of a plan she had to generate and build wealth among her friends and family and suggested that I/we come to her business, Tuft's Hats, to find out more about the concept .

I have had an entrepreneurial spirit for as long as I can remember. I feel that this spirit was fostered in me by community observation, reading books, magazines and periodicals that spoke to wealth building by investing in your God-given abilities and yourself.

After attending the "Business Concept" meeting and hearing the plan, I decided to get involved. After all, what could it hurt? I was already leading the youth department at church, working a full time job as an Assistant Executive Director of a non-profit housing organization, attending college with a full-load of classes and assisting in the rearing of three children plus taking care of my aging mother. While all of these activities are noble, none of it was helping to make me or my family financially secure.

I am credited with giving the organization its name **"Unique Enterprises"**. This came out of my thinking that we would be *unique* in our age diversity, *unique* in the fact that a mostly African-American Group could pool monies for the purpose of building and sharing resources and *unique* in how we approached the whole investment concept. If you *"...seek ye first the kingdom of God and His righteousness; then all the other things you desire will be given to you."* Matt. 6:33. My ambition is to ***"uniquely"*** use what God has provided for the purposes of obtaining and building wealth for this organization's members and family, to leave a legacy of African American Entrepreneurship and to "Take the whole Word to the whole world".

I was born in Yazoo City, Mississippi and raised in Oakland, CA. I am the eldest of two sons and am affectionately called Ronnie by family and friends. I got my start in entertainment by watching television variety shows which featured Sammy Davis Jr., Louis (Satchimo) Armstrong, James Brown and by participating in family talent contests.

I am a licensed and ordained minister that takes great pleasure in preaching, teaching and praising God. My ambition is to use my theatrical talents, education and life experience in ministry to quote the late Dr. J. Vernon McGee, "Take the whole Word to the whole world".

I have had parts in various television and film projects some of which include; "The Trash Art Project", "Golden Gate", ABC-TV's "Full House", "Nine Months", "Panther", "Angels In The Outfield" and the Academy Award winning "Mrs. Doubtfire". I am a founding member of the Bay Area's popular "HipHop/Street" dance act The Black Resurgents who sharpened their dance skills at various Arts Centers and have performed on stage with some of the biggest stars in the entertainment industry. I've also had experience as a production assistant, event producer and concert promoter, as well as participating in *2004's The Gospel Music Celebration* at B.B. Memorial Methodist Church, featuring the Oakland Interfaith Gospel Choir. I enjoy music and have sung with various local church choirs and participated with *The Black History Month Gospel Celebration*s in various years. My dramatic arts roles include the fairy godfather in "Black Cinderella", the character of Shorty in "Eli Haj Malik-The Malcolm X Story", Antioch Baptist Church's "SlabTown Convention". I also played 3 roles in the play "Green Pastures"; an Angel, Cain and Moses along with a number of singing engagements including The "Gospel Academy Awards" held at Oakland's Paramount Theater.

I am married to Robin and together we have three of my five children.

Robin - The Ties That Bind

I am "one of eight" of this partnership of *Unique Enterprises* and now retired Executive Assistant of a major hotel corporation. I have been married to William Randolph, the "Wild Card" for nearly forty years. We are proud parents and grandparents and take pride in having active involvement in this organization, our families, our community and our church.

When I was approached about becoming a member (partially because my husband was already a partner), I decided, "why not?". My personality was the type that would only allow space for the things that were passionate to me and based on that, I would have never given a thought, nor obligated my time, to an idea such as this. However, I had never been up close and personal within a body of people dedicated to obtaining financial gain and most definitely not within the African American community and I was curious, to say the least, at what it would be all about. I mean, could this really be done? Though it has been challenging, I'm proud to say I'm still here! My character is strong yet reserved at times, and I'm pretty much comfortable as an observer but I pushed past my comfort zone to participate in something almost non-existent in these times. Being a part of a group of people, whose personalities and knowledge were intimidating at times, excelled me in my own true personality, maturity and potential which also encouraged me to become more involved in this organization. It has been rewarding both individually and collectively. THE POWER OF EIGHT!

Jamal -The Marching Orders

I was in my thirties working in Logistics and Transportation and was always interested in real estate investments. However, I didn't have the finances or confidence to make that real estate investment a reality. So, when my fiancé shared with me an opportunity her college roommate's mother had about starting an investment group, I thought it was a good opportunity to realize a dream I'd been dreaming of for some time. Previously, I worked as a credit repair specialist repairing negative credit scores. I found that most of my clients were interested in repairing their credit to either purchase property or refinance their property. In the process, I realized the importance of owning real estate and how credit and money were the two main factors in the acquisition of purchasing property.

What I have learned from Unique so far, is basically our commitment to a greater goal and our commitment to the person next to you. What I believe Unique means to me up to this point, is that you cannot set aside other people that you love and respect in business. I feel that in business in order for it to work you have to love and respect the people you are in business with. When things get tight, things get personal. We were able to make sacrifices and I think things would have been impossible were it not for our faith in the Lord. I give Him praise for that, but I know we have been able to rally around each other because of our common goal and belief in the vision set before us.

I agree it has been difficult at times and has created times of hardship, but the blessing is we all made it through together. This taught me that you can always go to the next level when you stick together. With a common goal and the right people, amazing things can happen and as a result achieve the desired vision and goals for all of our futures. This group has grown together and learned a lot. We are still learning and I know we will be able to achieve great things as we move forward and continue to build on the foundation that has been created.

Currently my wife and I have been married for over 25 years and the Lord has blessed us with two beautiful children. Over the years we have purchased and sold properties and are looking forward to future real estate endeavors.

Madeline - The Faithful Scribe

I was given, by my partners, the name Faithful Scribe because of the many years I served as Secretary for Unique. I accepted this office as my dedicated and honored position in the group by recording a detailed and precise history of events in our meeting minutes. Today I am a first-time book co-author and recent empty-nester. My beloved husband Jamal and I have been married for over 25 years. We have two young adult children who are the jewels in the crown of our lives. I am also a quiet introverted woman who does not like the spotlight much. People say I have a very loyal heart both professionally and personally because I tend to persevere with people, even through the greatest of challenges. I've always had a heart for children with special needs due to having had an older brother with cerebral palsy. He, unfortunately, passed from esophageal cancer in 2005. Currently, I'm dedicated to working with children that have autism to honor the life of my brother and because I get my greatest fulfillment in making a difference in others' lives. My absolute joys are traveling, serving in my church home, spending time with family playing games, reading, and praise dancing on the beach.

Conclusion

As a group, we feel that it is our responsibility to leave a legacy and pass knowledge on to the next generation, we have made efforts to get this done. To this end we have sponsored events to share financial planning information with them and we also hosted musical events including them for just fun and relaxation. Most of all we get the opportunity to keep the dialogue going between both generations. We have found out that we can learn from them as much as we hope they are learning from us. After all, we expect them to take this investment club to a higher level and become bigger and better after we have shared our knowledge with them. We have continued to grow and sharpen our focus on real estate and stocks while increasing personal knowledge.

We are now eight people each with different personalities and different levels of education. In the end we come together to make up *Unique Enterprises* and forge forward to build a legacy of financial freedom for ourselves and generations to come.

References:

The King James Bible. (1722).

Hall, D. (n.d.). Ordinary People.

Whitaker, L. (1996). *The Beardstown Ladies' common-sense investment guide: How we beat the stock market-and how you can too*. Hyperion.

"Sense of A Goose" - attributed to Dr. Harry Clarke Noyes in

ARCS NEWS, Vol. 7, No. 1, January 1992*

© 2011, 2017, all rights reserved

Horatio R. Palmer. (n.d.). Yield Not to temptation.

*Oldest reference found, similar works by others

Notes:

Notes: